ignite

WINTER SPORTS

CURLING

Claire Throp

Raintree is an imprint of Capstone Global Library Limited, a company incorporated in England and Wales having its registered office at 7 Pilgrim Street, London, EC4V 6LB – Registered company number: 6695582

To contact Raintree please phone 0845 6044371, fax + 44 (0) 1865 312263, or email myorders@raintreepublishers.co.uk. Customers from outside the UK please telephone +44 1865 312262.

Text © Capstone Global Library Limited 2014
First published in paperback in 2014
The moral rights of the proprietor have been asserted.

Edited by Adam Miller, Nancy Dickmann, and John-Paul Wilkins
Designed by Richard Parker and Ken Vail Graphic Design
Picture research by Elizabeth Alexander
Originated by Capstone Global Library Ltd
Production by Vicki Fitzgerald
Printed and bound in China by Leo Paper Products Ltd

ISBN 978 1 406 26029 8
17 16 15 14 13
10 9 8 7 6 5 4 3 2 1

British Library Cataloguing in Publication Data
Throp, Claire.
Curling. -- (Winter Sports)
A full catalogue record for this book is available from the British Library.

Acknowledgements
We would like to thank the following for permission to reproduce photographs: Alamy pp. 6 (© Mary Evans Picture Library), 15 (© Andrew Walmsley), 16 (© Tom Wallace/Minneapolis Star Tribune/ZUMAPRESS. Com), 17, 18, 30 (© epa european pressphoto agency b.v.), 24 (© Andres Rodriguez), 27 (© PCN Photography), 31 (© Hipix), 32 (© George S de Blonsky), 38 (© All Canada Photos), 39 (© IDEAL STOCK), 40 (© photomadnz), 41 (© CanStock Images); Corbis pp. 4 (© Don Feria/isiphotos.com), 5 (© Barry Lewis/In Pictures), 7 (© Hulton-Deutsch Collection), 13 bottom (© Jean-Christophe Bott/epa); Getty Images pp. 10 (Bryn Lennon), 11 (Claus Andersen), 12 (Robyn Beck/AFP), 19 (Fabrice Coffrini/AFP), 20, 37 (Cameron Spencer), 23, 28, 34 (John MACDOUGALL/AFP), 25 (Claus Fisker/AFP), 29 (Saeed Khan/AFP), 35 (Clive Rose), 36 (Toshifumi Kitamura/AFP); iStockphoto p. 9 (© The Power of Forever Photography); Press Association Images pp. 8 (Robert F. Bukaty/AP), 22 (PA Wire/PA Archive), 26 (Robert Bukaty/AP); Reuters p. 33 (Russell Cheyne); Shutterstock pp. imprint page (© Corepics VOF), 9 inset (© Carolina K. Smith, M.D.), 13 top (© Anton Balazh), 14 (© Bork), 21, 44-45 (© Jerry Zitterman), 42-43 (© Pashin Georgiy), 47 (© Gemenacom).

Design features reproduced with permission of Shutterstock (© A'lya, © Allgusak, © Bork, © Eky Studio, © LehaKoK, © Lonely, © Max Sudakov, © Myrtilleshop, © Nicemonkey, © Nik Merkulov, © Number One, © secondcorner, © Tanchic, © Vadim Georgiev).

Cover photo of Northern Ontario skip Brad Jacobs throwing a rock in a game against Team Manitoba in the Tim Hortons Brier Canadian Men's Curling Championship on 7 March, 2011 at the John Labatt Centre in London, Canada, reproduced with permission of Getty Images (Claus Andersen).

Every effort has been made to contact copyright holders of material reproduced in this book. Any omissions will be rectified in subsequent printings if notice is given to the publisher.

CONTENTS

Some words are shown in bold, **like this**. You can find out what they mean by looking in the glossary.

CURLING: A FASCINATING SPORT

It is Canada versus Norway in the men's curling final at the 2002 Winter Olympics. Canada are clear favourites to win. However, at the final **end** the teams are tied. Canada still has the last stone advantage and are likely to win. Then Norway plays an almost perfect end, forcing a mistake from the Canadians. Norway wins the gold medal.

Curling is known as…

Curling is similar to playing bowls on ice. The aim is to slide stones towards the centre of a target and the stones that end up closest to the centre win points. The name 'curling' comes from the way that the stone curls across the ice.

Curling is sometimes known as "chess on ice". This is because **strategy** plays such an important role in the game. Working out the path and placement of a stone takes a lot of planning. It is also known as the "roaring game" because of the noise the stone makes as it moves across the ice.

Concentration is important when a player is about to deliver a stone.

Which are the top teams?

Curling is played in 49 countries, including the UK, the United States, Canada, Norway, Sweden, and China. The game is particularly popular in Canada and they dominate the men's game. Great Britain and Norway are also top men's teams. Sweden and Canada are the top women's teams.

> "Curling is getting a little bit more popular because of the Olympics. We want to be able to promote the sport because it's not very well known."
>
> – Cassie Johnson, US **skip**

Curling is mainly played indoors nowadays but if it is cold enough, it can still be played outside.

This book will look at some basic rules of curling and how to play. It will also focus on the major championships and some of the best known players.

A HISTORY OF CURLING

Many believe curling began in Scotland as the first written mention of curling comes from Scotland, in 1540. Others think that curling was first played in the Low Countries (now the Netherlands, Belgium, and Luxembourg). Artist Pieter Breughel included Dutch peasants playing a game that looks like curling in two of his paintings dated 1565. There was trade between Britain and the Low Countries at this time, but it is not certain which country introduced the game to the other.

NO WAY!

The oldest known curling stone – the Stirling Stone – was found in Dunblane in Scotland. It has '1511' marked on the side. It's about half the size of a modern curling stone and square rather than round.

When the game was first played, the stones used were usually flat-bottomed stones from rivers. Later, Scottish weavers used to play during their breaks and used heavy weights from the weaving machinery with handles attached. Curling was played by friends and work colleagues in Scotland for many years before curling clubs began to form around the second half of the 18th century. By the 1830s, there were calls for a national organization to standardize the rules. The Grand Caledonian Curling Club (later the Royal Caledonian Curling Club) became the **governing body**, set up in 1838.

This woman was a competitor in the first Scottish outdoor tournament of 1959.

Early competitions

Curling was first played at the Olympics in 1924 (see page 27), while the Scotch Cup is considered the first world championship. It was first held in Scotland in 1959 between teams from Scotland and Canada. A Canadian team won. The World Championships soon became an established part of international competition, and Olympic participation came in 1998. Other tournaments have been added over the years, including junior and wheelchair championships.

THE BASICS

The aim of curling is to get your stones closer to the **tee** than the other team in order to win points. The team with the most points wins. The area on which a curling game is played is called the **curling sheet**.

The ice

While skaters need wet ice so their skates can move smoothly over it, curlers need to have a dry surface with a 'pebble' of water droplets on top. Before a game, an ice technician uses a **pebbling** machine that sprays a fine mist of hot water over the flat ice surface. Soon, there is a layer of tiny bumps on the surface of the ice. These mean that the running edge on the bottom of each stone has minimal contact with the flat ice, allowing it to glide smoothly. As a game goes on and the pebble wears down, stones start to travel less distance and curl more.

An ice technician prepares the ice for play with a pebbling machine.

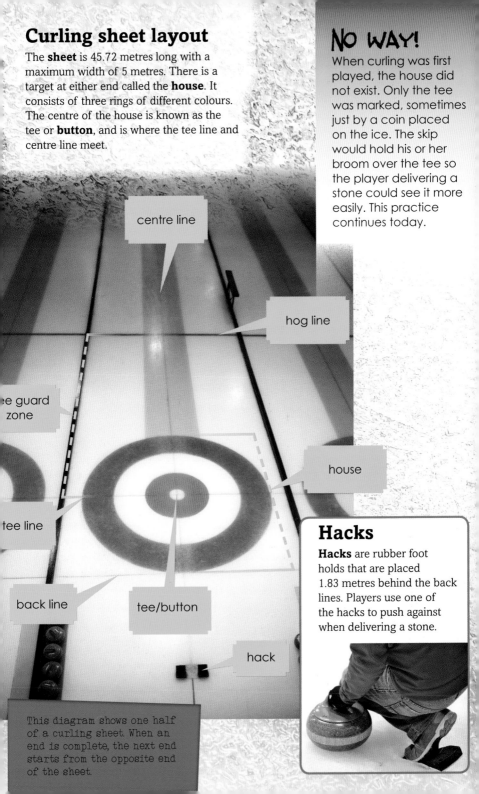

Curling sheet layout

The **sheet** is 45.72 metres long with a maximum width of 5 metres. There is a target at either end called the **house**. It consists of three rings of different colours. The centre of the house is known as the tee or **button**, and is where the tee line and centre line meet.

NO WAY!

When curling was first played, the house did not exist. Only the tee was marked, sometimes just by a coin placed on the ice. The skip would hold his or her broom over the tee so the player delivering a stone could see it more easily. This practice continues today.

centre line

hog line

ee guard zone

house

tee line

back line

tee/button

hack

Hacks

Hacks are rubber foot holds that are placed 1.83 metres behind the back lines. Players use one of the hacks to push against when delivering a stone.

This diagram shows one half of a curling sheet. When an end is complete, the next end starts from the opposite end of the sheet.

The team

A curling team is known as a **rink**. It is made up of four players: lead, second, third, and the skip. The lead delivers the first and second stones, the second delivers the third and fourth stones, and third or vice skip delivers the fifth and sixth stones. The last two stones are delivered by the skip, or captain, of the team. Each player alternates with their equivalent on the opposing team. One of the most important parts of curling is how well the team works together. This helps the team to run smoothly and often brings success.

CASSIE JOHNSON

Born: 30 October 1981 in Bemidji, USA
Nationality: American
Known for: silver medal winner at the 2005 World Championships; skip of USA team at 2006 Winter Olympics
Interesting fact: Cassie's sister, Jamie, also plays on the US curling team

Against the clock

A game is made up of 8 or 10 ends played against the clock. Each team has 73 minutes to complete all 10 ends (59 minutes to complete 8 ends) and there is a five-minute break after five ends. If a team goes over this time limit, they lose the game.

house

Glossary of terms

button   centre of the house and also known as the tee; stones closest to the button win the points

curling sheet   place where the game is played

end   period of time during which each player throws two stones. Games have either 8 or 10 ends.

hog line   line that goes across the width of the curling sheet. Players must release the stone before they reach this line.

house   area within the circles at each end of the curling sheet

rink   team or the name of the place where curling is played (ice rink)

skip   captain of the team

tee line   line that goes across the width of the curling sheet, passing through the centre of the tee and parallel to the hog line

The free guard rule

The **free guard zone** is the area between the **hog line** and tee line, but not including the house. The free guard rule states that any stones in the free guard zone cannot be knocked out of play by an opponent's stone until the first two stones from each side have been delivered. If they are knocked out, then they are replaced and the stone that hit them is taken out of play.

Measuring devices, like this one, measure the distance from the nearest part of the stone to the tee.

Scoring

Each stone that is within the house and closer to the button than the opposition's stones wins a point. Only one team can score in each end. If the score is even after ten ends, an extra end is played. Whichever team scores first wins. Sometimes it can be difficult to tell which team's stone is the closest to the button when an end finishes, so a measuring device is used.

No Way!

Russ Howard, a Canadian skip, caused a change in rules because he'd gone hoarse during the 1989 **Brier** while yelling instructions. He started using a two-way radio. The match officials asked him not to use the radio in the next match. However, there was nothing in the rules to say radios weren't allowed, so Howard used it again in the following match. Officials were forced to change the rules before the next round to state that no radios would be allowed. It was the first time that a new rule had been introduced in the middle of a competition.

The skip is the person who leads the team and decides strategy.

EQUIPMENT

Curling stones are made from a strong rock called granite. They each weigh 19.1 kilograms and have a plastic handle on top. A ring, called the running edge, on the bottom of the stone, is the only part of the stone to touch the ice. Apart from the striking band (a band of granite in the middle of the stone) and the running edge, the rest of the stone is highly polished. When the striking band hits another stone, it forces it to move in the opposite direction – good for getting rid of an opponent's stone.

handle

striking band

Curling stones used in the Olympics come from the Scottish island of Ailsa Craig and are sometimes known as Ailsas. The island is now a reserve for the Royal Society for the Protection of Birds (RSPB), and although blasting is forbidden, loose rocks are still taken to make curling stones. Other stones are made from granite quarried in Trefor, Wales.

The unique properties of Ailsa Craig granite make it perfect for curling stones.

Brushes

A brush or broom is an essential piece of equipment for any curler. Everyone in the team except the skip uses a brush to sweep. They all use the brush for balance when delivering a stone. Originally, a hog- or horse-hair brush was used but most curlers now use brushes with **synthetic** pads.

NO WAY!

Using a broom to sweep the ice in front of a stone comes from the sport originally being played on a frozen lake, and players having to sweep away the snow before they could deliver a shot. Thankfully, the players don't have to deal with snow anymore!

Clothing

As the game of curling is played on ice, warm clothing is usually necessary! The clothes should be comfortable to wear. There are trousers especially designed for curling. They need to be stretchy to allow for a big range of movement, particularly when delivering a stone. They look very similar to tracksuit bottoms. Gloves are also worn and are usually made of calf or deer skin. They need to fit well, or they may cause blisters from all the **sweeping**. Some players wear mittens but most find gloves are better for gripping the brush.

Slider shoes have smooth pads so they can glide across the ice.

Shoes

The most important thing to get is the right type of shoes. When delivering a stone, one foot needs to be able to slide along the ice. The bottom of the shoe needs to be covered in a low-friction material, such as Teflon. This shoe needs to be protected when not on the ice as it is easily damaged. Some players use a slider that slips on to the bottom of the shoe and can be removed easily when they step off the ice. The other shoe needs to be able to grip the ice so it usually has a rubber sole that is non-slip.